great example
to me. I'm so
grateful to be
your sister + in
your family.

All my love,

Julie
Layden

Heathers, I saw this while shopping for your Mom, and thought it was so cute, I hope you enjoy it. Julie

THE LITTLE BOOK OF big ideas ABOUT Mothers

Linda J. Eyre

EAGLE
GATE

Visit us at www.deseretbook.com

Library of Congress Catalog Card Number 00-136057

ISBN 1-57345-923-2

Printed in Mexico   18961-6794

10   9   8   7   6   5   4   3   2   1

M is for Motherhood.

No question about it, when we seek a suitable symbol for all that mother is and does, M qualifies. In its original design it is perfect—squares off properly, wide as it is high, like a woman who juggles children in the womb, cuddled in arms, babe on her back, child in hand, with packages and purse. Its lipless sound is universally formed inside of the mouth, which students of phonetics label a "bilabial nasal consonant." And, miraculously, in any language, "Mama" is often baby's first sound.

Motherhood is God's way of blessing the world with women who will fulfill such a need. Motherhood carries with it the privileges of a partnership with Heavenly Father and the duty to guide and love his eternal spirit children during their mortal stay on earth.

Motherhood is one of the better things to happen to anyone. Even if the experience is vicarious as a substitute or surrogate, it feels great to nurture another human being along the way in life. As members of a generation bombarded by signs, signals, squalls, road construction, and the swiftest passage of time ever struggled through, we

need mothers and we need mothering. We need someone who will ease the load, meet the crisis, give the hug, be the Good Samaritan, testify and teach of truth, love us, and comfort us.

To mothers is given the flaming torch that helps light the world. If anyone understands this calling, it is Linda Eyre. This little book of big ideas about mothers is filled with her collection of thoughts and personal perspective on this beautiful and important subject. Enjoy it, and feel blessed.

Elaine Cannon

ℰℬ

[Homemaking] is surely in reality the

most important work in the world.

What do ships, railways, mines, cars, and

government, etc. exist for except that

people may be fed, warmed, and safe in

their own homes? . . . [The homemaker's]

job is one for which all others exist.

—C. S. Lewis

Of all the careers that women may be

involved in, a career as a mother is undoubtedly

the most important. In today's world, we find

that motherhood is no less demanding or time

consuming than running a large corporation.

The most successful homes are run by mothers

who take their careers as seriously as any top

executive. Instead of dealing with making a

product profitable, however, we are dealing with

making profit of human lives. An organized plan

with a mission statement and specific goals is

more important to a mother who wants to create

a great family than it is to an executive who

wants to create a great company.

LOVE DOESN'T JUST SIT THERE, LIKE A STONE.

IT HAS TO BE MADE, LIKE BREAD;

REMADE ALL THE TIME, MADE NEW.

—URSULA K. LEGUIN

A young mother recounts: "It was one of the worst days of my life. The washing machine broke down, the telephone kept ringing, my head ached, and the mail carrier brought a bill I had no money to pay. Almost to the breaking point, I lifted my one-year-old into his high chair, leaned my head against the tray, and began to cry. Without a word, my son took his pacifier out of his mouth and stuck it in mine."

If I had any advice for mothers it would be this from author Iris Krasnow: "Be There. . . . I know that I'm fortunate to be in a profession and marriage that allows me to spend most of each day near my children. But Being There isn't about money or even about staying home full-time. It's about an emotional and spiritual

shift, of succumbing to Being Where You
Are When You Are, and Being There as
much as possible. It's about crouching on
the floor and getting delirious over the
praying mantis your son just caught instead
of perusing a fax [or filling the dishwasher]
while he is yelling for your attention and
you distractedly say over your shoulder:
'Oh, honey, isn't that a pretty bug.' It's
about being attuned enough to notice when
your kid's eyes shine so you can make your
eyes shine back."

A distraught mother, dealing with an adopted daughter who had broken her heart with her behavior and had moved out of the house, approached her daughter on one of her infrequent visits home. She looked deep into her daughter's heavily made-up face, complete with black lipstick and multiple piercings in each ear, and asked, "Jenny, has it ever occurred to you that a loving Heavenly Father sent you to us so that you could learn how to conduct your life in a way that would make you happy?" Her rebellious daughter answered with equal sincerity and without malice, "Mother, has it ever occurred to you that I was sent to you so that you could learn how to love *all* people, no matter how they act?"

As a mother, visualize yourself as being involved in the world's most important endeavor. You are shaping lives, breeding self-confidence, discovering talent, directing the people you love most toward making contributions. You are doing your part in a grassroots way to strengthen the crumbling American family unit, which forms the true foundation of a great society.

EVERY MOTHER IS LIKE MOSES.

SHE DOES NOT ENTER THE PROMISED LAND.

SHE PREPARES A WORLD SHE WILL NOT SEE.

—POPE PAUL VI

We salute our sisters for the joy that is theirs as they rejoice in a baby's first smile and as they listen with eager ear to a child's first day at school. . . . Women, more quickly than others, will understand the possible dangers when the word *self* is militantly placed before other words like *fulfillment*. They rock a sobbing child without wondering if today's world is passing them by because they know they hold tomorrow tightly in their arms.

—NEAL A. MAXWELL

INSTEAD OF ALWAYS TRYING

TO KEEP YOUR KIDS OUT OF

THE MUD PUDDLES, TRY

JUMPING IN WITH THEM!

OTHERHOOD IS THE GREAT EQUALIZER. WHETHER WE LIVE IN BULGARIA OR KENTUCKY, WHETHER WE RESIDE IN A MANSION OR A GRASS HUT, WHETHER WE HAVE ONE CHILD OR FIFTEEN, WE ALL HAVE THE SAME GOAL: TO HELP OUR CHILDREN TO REACH THE GREATNESS WITHIN THEM AND TO SURVIVE THE PROCESS OURSELVES. AND IN THE COURSE, A MAGICAL THING HAPPENS: WE ACTUALLY BECOME BETTER FOR THE WEAR!

*The hardest part
of being a mother
is taking care of
yourself!*

The ultimate lesson all of us have

to learn is *unconditional love*,

which includes not only others

but ourselves as well.

—Elisabeth Kubler-Ross

THOSE WHO LAUGH . . . LAST.

One of the best things a mother can bring to her family is education. Formal education is important, but in our world of modern technology there is also great potential to educate ourselves at home. The most exciting part of mothering is realizing that there is something new to learn every day. Henry Ward Beecher said, "The mother's heart is the child's schoolroom." Our wisdom and learning is the basis of our children's education not only while they are children, but for their children and for many generations to come.

An interesting secret weapon for changing behavior when dealing with any problem that a child may be experiencing is one we don't remember often enough because it's the exact opposite of our natural instinct: Praise.

A MOTHER IS NOT A PERSON TO

LEAN ON BUT A PERSON TO MAKE

LEANING UNNECESSARY.

—DOROTHY CANFIELD FISHER

"She broke the bread into two fragments and gave them to the children, who ate with avidity.

'She hath kept none for herself,' grumbled the Sergeant.

'Because she is not hungry,' said a soldier.

'Because she is a mother,' said the Sergeant."

—Victor Hugo

Angry, annoyed, frustrated, and exasperated, my tires screeched as I pulled up to the school curb for the second time that week with a child who couldn't find his shoes and was late for school. Completely unaware of my mental state, my blue-eyed, right-brained seven-year-old son turned to me just as he reached for the door handle and asked, "Mom, did you see the way the sunlight reflected off the water in that manhole cover on the way down here?"

A great moment for a paradigm shift!

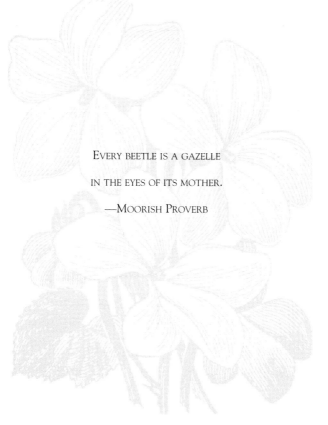

EVERY BEETLE IS A GAZELLE

IN THE EYES OF ITS MOTHER.

—MOORISH PROVERB

All that I am or hope to be I owe to my angel mother. I remember my mother's prayers and they have always followed me. They have clung to me all my life.

—ABRAHAM LINCOLN

It might help us all to know that there

are a lot of moms who are super, but

there are no "Super Moms."

SOME ARE KISSING MOTHERS

AND SOME ARE SCOLDING

MOTHERS, BUT IT IS LOVE JUST

THE SAME, AND MOST MOTHERS

KISS AND SCOLD TOGETHER.

—PEARL S. BUCK

What a wonderful thing is the mind of a two-year-old, well trained in the art of prayer by a loving mother who is always praying for safety! After having driven past the Salt Lake Temple on an errand that day, Nathan's bedtime prayer included: "Please help the angel Moroni to get down safely."

They say that man is mighty;

He governs land and sea,

He wields a might scepter

O'er lesser powers that be.

But a mightier power and stronger

Man from his throne has hurled,

For the hand that rocks the cradle

Is the hand that rules the world.

—William Ross Wallace

THE GREATER PART OF OUR HAPPINESS OR

MISERY DEPENDS ON OUR DISPOSITIONS

AND NOT ON OUR CIRCUMSTANCES.

—FIRST LADY MARTHA WASHINGTON

If you're burned-out on whining, crying, feeding, bribing, refereeing, and driving to ballet, soccer, and piano lessons with no thanks, find some way to get away from it all for twenty-four hours. Rent a motel room for twenty-four hours and *think, plan, revise, explore, recommit, visualize the future, set goals for yourself and each child.* You'll be amazed at how much better your life is and how much cuter the kids are when you get home!

INSTEAD OF WORRYING ABOUT

ORGANIZING OUR CHILDREN'S TIME

WITH EVERY IMAGINABLE EXPERIENCE

TO DEVELOP EVERY POSSIBLE TALENT,

PERHAPS WE MOTHERS SHOULD

WORRY MORE ABOUT ALLOWING OUR

CHILDREN TO HAVE MORE EXPERIENCE

WITH UNORGANIZED TIME AND SPACE.

A wise mother is neither cocky nor proud because she knows the school principal may call at any minute to report that her child has just driven a motorcycle through the gymnasium.

—Mary Kay Blakely

I believe that the key to relieving a great
deal of stress for mothers is to simplify. As
Thoreau so aptly puts it, "Our life is frittered
away with detail. . . . Simplify, simplify."

The most important of the Lord's work

that you will ever do will be the work you

do within the walls of your own home.

—Harold B. Lee

Now they never had fought, yet they did not fear death; and they did think more upon the liberty of their fathers than they did upon their lives; yea, they had been taught by their mothers, that if they did not doubt, God would deliver them.

—ALMA 56:47

They'll be gone before you
know it. The fingerprints on the
wall appear higher and higher.
Then suddenly they disappear.

—Dorothy Evslin

Write down a list of all the things you'd

like to do at Christmas. Then mark each

one with VI (very important), SI (some-

what important), or TD (trivial detail).

Plan exactly when to do the VIs. Fit the

SIs in if you can . . . and forget the TDs.

In the sheltered simplicity of the first days

after a baby is born, one sees again the

magical closed circle, the miraculous sense

of two people existing only for each other.

—Anne Morrow Lindbergh

IF YOU'VE HAD A HORRENDOUS DAY WHICH

MAY HAVE INCLUDED CRISIS AFTER CRISIS, ANGRY

WORDS, DINNERTIME CHAOS, LOST HOMEWORK,

LOTS OF TIME DEALING WITH "TIME OUT," OR THE

FRUSTRATIONS OF POTTY TRAINING, AND YOU

WANT TO RELIEVE THE TENSION AND RESTORE

YOUR INNER PEACE, TIPTOE INTO YOUR CHILDREN'S

ROOMS AND WATCH THEM SLEEP.

Making the decision to have a

child—it's momentous. It is to

decide forever to have your heart go

walking around outside your body.

—Elizabeth Stone

hildren are not lumps of clay that a mother can mold and shape into whatever she thinks would be best. They are seedlings . . . already pears, pines, or petunias. As gardeners, we can add only sunshine, water, fertilizer, time, and love in order to make that growing plant the most beautiful specimen of what it was intended to be.

Becoming a mother makes you the mother of all children. From now on each wounded, abandoned, frightened child is yours. You live in the suffering mothers of every race and creed and weep with them. You long to comfort all who are desolate.

—Charlotte Gray

The only thing
that's ever the same
about mothering
is that every child
is different.

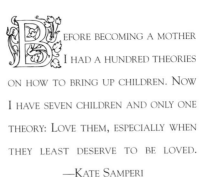

BEFORE BECOMING A MOTHER I HAD A HUNDRED THEORIES ON HOW TO BRING UP CHILDREN. NOW I HAVE SEVEN CHILDREN AND ONLY ONE THEORY: LOVE THEM, ESPECIALLY WHEN THEY LEAST DESERVE TO BE LOVED.

—KATE SAMPERI

The woman . . . who deserts the cradle in

order to help defend civilization against

the barbarians may well later meet, among

the barbarians, her own neglected child.

—Neal A. Maxwell

Teenagers are often like the werewolves we meet in the movies . . . good, kind, and reasonable people, who, when the moon comes up, sprout long hideous fangs, straggly hair on arms and cheeks, complete with wild piercing eyes that tell us that they are no longer really in control of themselves. The best part is that in the morning, when the moon has set, these wild creatures turn back into wonderful people, with torn clothes and dirt under their fingernails, feeling much better and wondering what on earth happened to them.

CONTRARY TO POPULAR BELIEF, MOTHERS CAN MAKE MISTAKES. TWO OF THE MOST IMPORTANT WORDS A MOTHER CAN SAY ARE, "I'M SORRY." THEN EXPLAIN WHY YOU ACTED AS YOU DID. THE BEST REWARD FOR ADMITTING YOUR HUMANNESS IS AN OCCASIONAL NOTE ON YOUR PILLOW AFTER A HARD DAY WITH A CHILD, WITH AN APOLOGY FOR *THEIR* BAD BEHAVIOR.

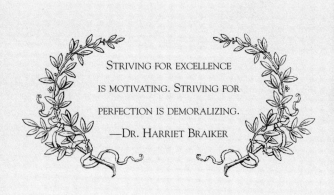

STRIVING FOR EXCELLENCE
IS MOTIVATING. STRIVING FOR
PERFECTION IS DEMORALIZING.
—DR. HARRIET BRAIKER

The worst part about changing your husband and your children is that the first one to change has to be you!

The great anchor of my motherhood and our household has been the influence of our dear Savior Jesus Christ. His picture is proudly displayed in each child's room and our daily behavior is driven by our desire to be more like him. C. S. Lewis sculpted my feelings perfectly when he said, "I believe in Jesus Christ just as I believe in the rising sun; not because I can see it, but because of it, I can see everything else."

With the birth of son after son, I was
[moved] beyond the obsessive, self-analysis
that had forever racked my heart.
Enmeshed in a world of little things and
little people, I was slammed into the
moment with such ferocity and velocity
that now it's all there is. My kids have
captured me, and I am surrendering.
I am no longer mine; I am theirs.

—Iris Krasnow

Life as a mother would be pretty dreary if it weren't for those paydays when your child gives you a poem for your birthday or writes you a note thanking you for your painstaking help on a science project:

From a delightful eight-year-old:

You are a butuful spontaneous horse who always has

to work for her babies.

You are sophisticated and sensative. You have the

sweetest smile.

Happy Birthday

Love, Talmadge

From a stoic ten-year-old:

Dear Mom,

Thank you for getting the eye balls for us. We couldn't

have done it without you. Thanks for going out so far

to get them for us.

Love, Josh

Cleaning and scrubbing

Can wait 'til tomorrow

For babies grow up,

We've learned to our sorrow.

So quiet down cobwebs,

Dust, go to sleep

I'm rocking my baby,

And babies don't keep.

—ANONYMOUS

If you ask your kids, "How was your day?" when they get home from school, you'll probably get a one-word answer, "Fine." If you ask, "What was the best thing that happened to you today?" or "If you could have done one thing differently today, what would it be?" or "What was the most interesting thing that you learned today?" you might be amazed at the answers you get!

It's not what happens in the White

House that will change our society.

It's what happens in your house.

—Barbara Bush

A successful mother is not a soloist alone on a stage. Rather, she is part of a choral group made up of her children's father, extended family, friends, and her children. She may be the director of the group and she may be called upon to do quite a few solo parts. But she must help all members of the group to make a contribution. The mother can help everyone in the group to learn their own distinct part, listen carefully to the others, find the harmonies, and enjoy the beautiful result.

—Saren Eyre

about the author

Linda J. Eyre is a mother of nine, a writer, and a speaker, but she characterizes herself as a learner. She and her husband, Richard, created the Joy School programs employed by thousands across the nation. Their family resides in Salt Lake City, Utah, and Washington, D.C.

ISBN 1-57345-923-2

50795

EAN

9 781573 459235

SKU 4132209 U.S. $7.95